DARKNESS AND LIGHT

MYSTICISM AND MODERN MAN

DARKNESS AND LIGHT

Selections from St. John of the Cross

edited by Catharine Hughes

Sheed & Ward · New York

The quotations are from *The Complete Works of St. John of the Cross,* translated and edited by E. Allison Peers, 3 vols. (Westminster, Maryland: The Newman Press, 1935); *Complete Works of St. John of the Cross,* translated by David Lewis (London: Longman, Green, Longman, Roberts and Green, 1864); and *St. John of the Cross* by Bruno de Jesus-Marie, O.D.C. (New York: Sheed and Ward).

Library of Congress Cataloging in Publication Data

Juan de la Cruz, Saint, 1542-1591.
  Darkness and light.

  (Mysticism and modern man)
  1. Catholic Church—Collected works.   2. Theology—Collected works—16th century.   3. Mysticism—Collected works.   I. Hughes, Catharine, 1935-   ed.   II. Title.
[BX890.J62413 1972]   149'.3   72-6269
ISBN 0-8362-0502-2

Copyright © 1972 by Sheed and Ward, Inc.

Manufactured in the United States of America

DARKNESS AND LIGHT

My Beloved is the mountains,
The solitary wooded valleys,
The strange islands,
The roaring torrents,
The whisper of the amorous gales;
The tranquil night
At the approaches of the dawn,
The silent music,
The murmuring solitude,
The supper which revives, and enkindles love.

Where there is no love, put love and you will find love.

Come, my brethren, and see how these little animals, God's creatures, praise Him. Lift up your minds; and, since creatures without reason or intelligence do so, have we not a far greater obligation to praise Him?

For all that in the way of sense
I may obtain on earth,
And all I may understand—
However high it may be—

For all grace and beauty—
Never will I lose myself;
But only for that I know not,
Which may happily be found.

The night's deep peaceful mood,
And dim approaching dawn's first orient rays;
The singing solitude,
A symphony of praise.

The eyes of a moth avail it but little because the attractions of the beauty of light leads it to be consumed in the flame.

Always seek for preference
not the easiest but the hardest;
not the most charming but the most boring;

not what pleases but what repels;
not what consoles but rather what afflicts;
not what saves us trouble but what gives us trouble;

not the most but the least;
not the highest and most precious but the
   lowest and most despised;

9

not the desire of something but the non-desire; do not seek what is better in things but what is worse, and for Jesus Christ put yourself in denudation, emptiness, and renunciation of all that exists in this world.

10

What dost thou then ask for, what dost thou seek for, O my soul? All is thine, all is for thee, do not take less, nor rest with the crumbs which fall from the table of thy Father. Go forth and exult in thy glory, hide thyself in it, and rejoice, and thou shalt obtain all the desires of thy heart.

What proportion can there be between the creature and the Creator, the sensual and the spiritual, the visible and the invisible, the passing and the eternal, between pure, spiritual, heavenly food and mere sensual food of the senses, between the nakedness of Christ and attachment to anything?

All the liberty and power of the world, compared with the Power and Liberty of the Spirit of God, is but supreme slavery, wretchedness, and captivity.

I am not made for dealing with the world.

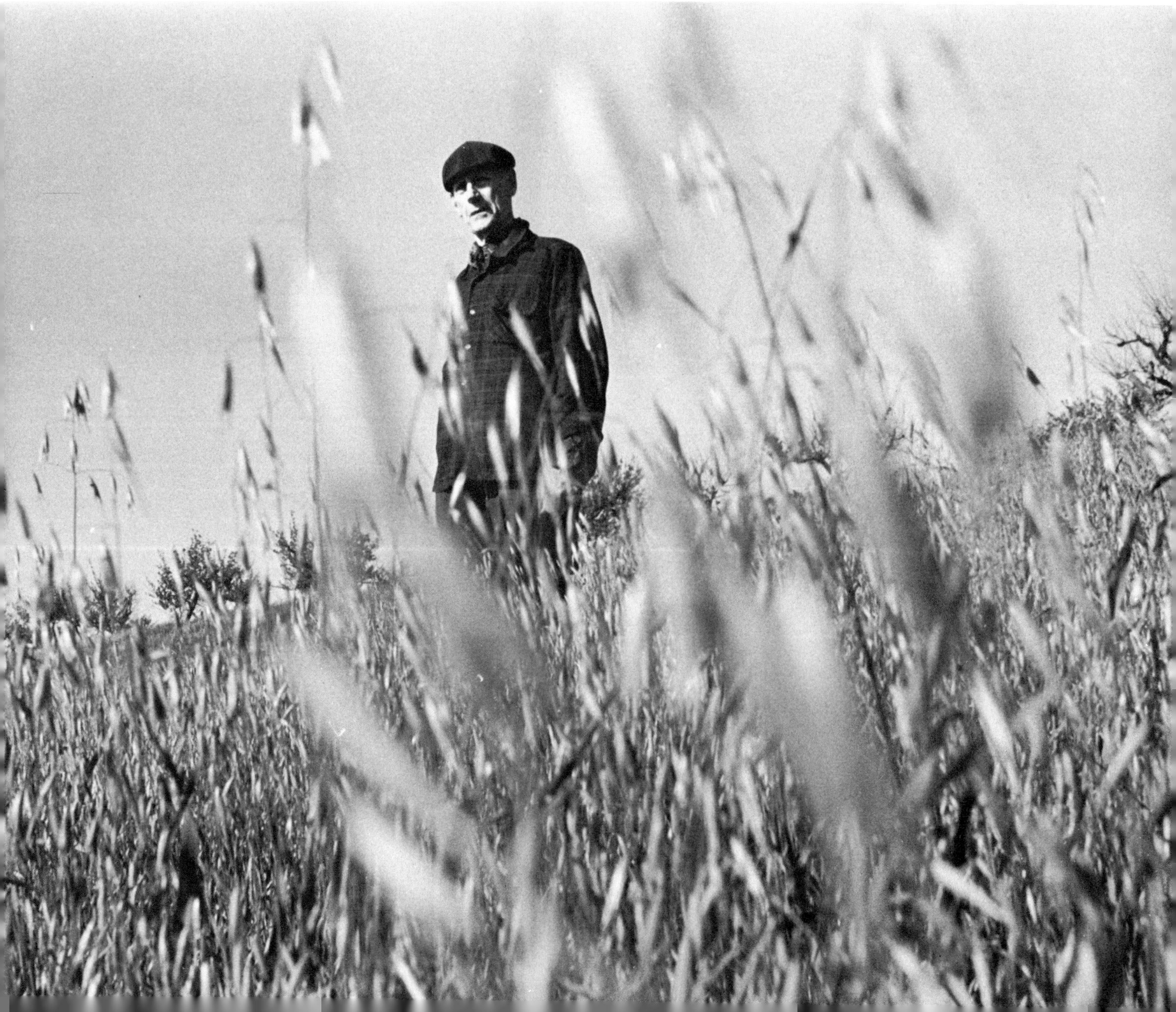

All the wisdom of the world, and all human cunning, compared with the infinite Wisdom of God, is simple and supreme ignorance, "for the wisdom of this world is foolishness with God." . . . They alone attain to Divine Wisdom who, like children and ignorant ones, lay aside their own wisdom, and serve God in Love.

The heavens are mine, the earth is mine
and the nations are mine; mine are the just,
and the sinners are mine; mine are the
angels, the Mother of God, and all things
are mine; God Himself is mine and for me,
because Christ is mine, and all for me.

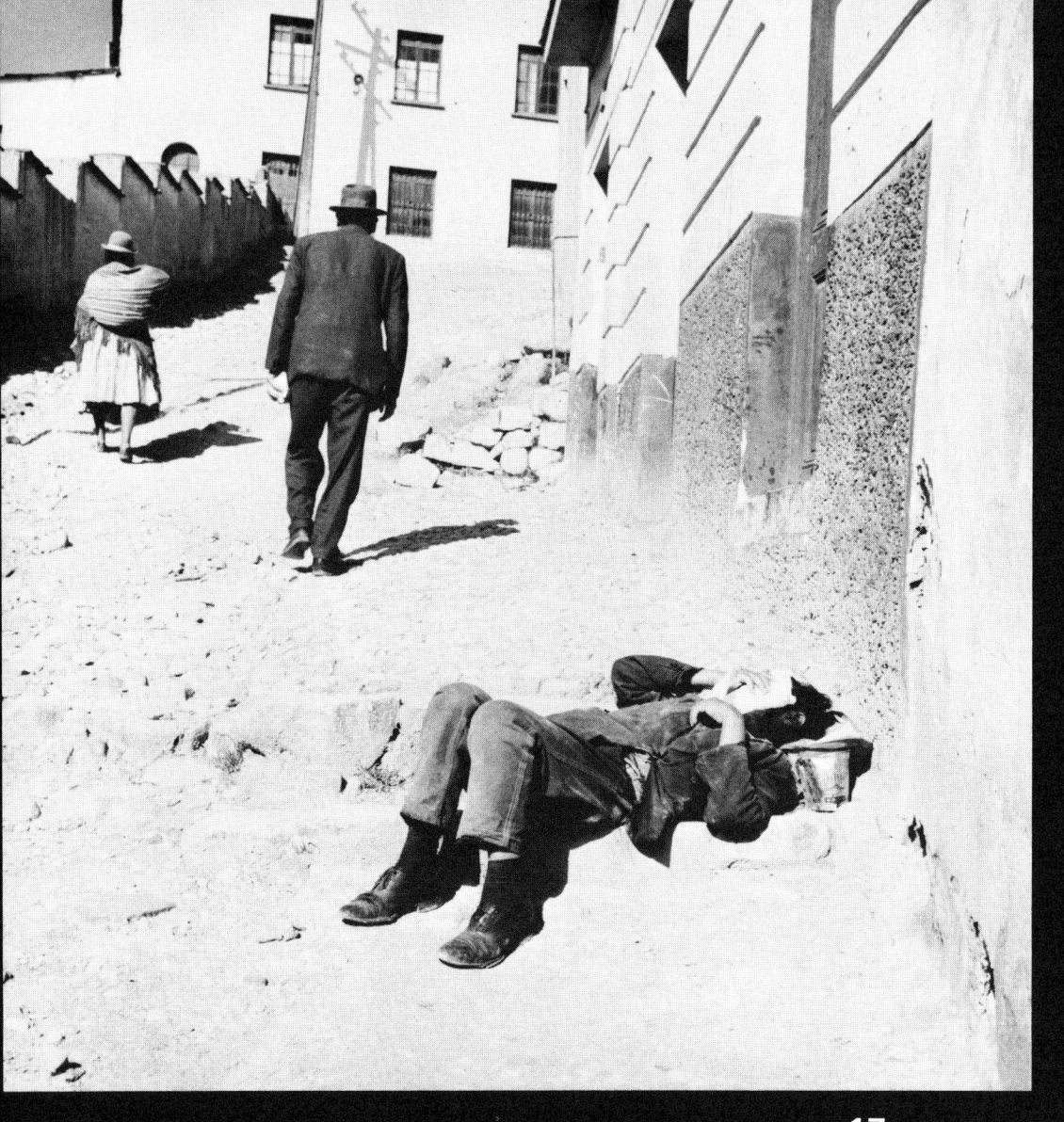

Thou hastenest joyfully and lovingly, O Lord, to raise up him who has offended Thee, but I make no haste to honor and raise him up who has offended me.

In the evening of this life, you will be examined
upon Love.

Upon love's chase, I went my way,
Not void of hope, began to fly,
And soar'd aloft, so high, so high,
That in the end I reach'd my prey.

In ways that none can e'er explain
I made a thousand flights in one,
For he that hopes to reach the sun
His heart's desire shall surely gain.
Naught had I hoped for but this day
And hope impell'd me up to fly.
I soared aloft so high, so high,
that in the end I reach'd my prey.

He that loves not his neighbor abhors God.

Think not that, because in yonder man there shine not the virtues which thou hast in mind, he will not be precious in God's sight for that which thou hast not in mind.

The soul that walks in love wearies not, neither is wearied.

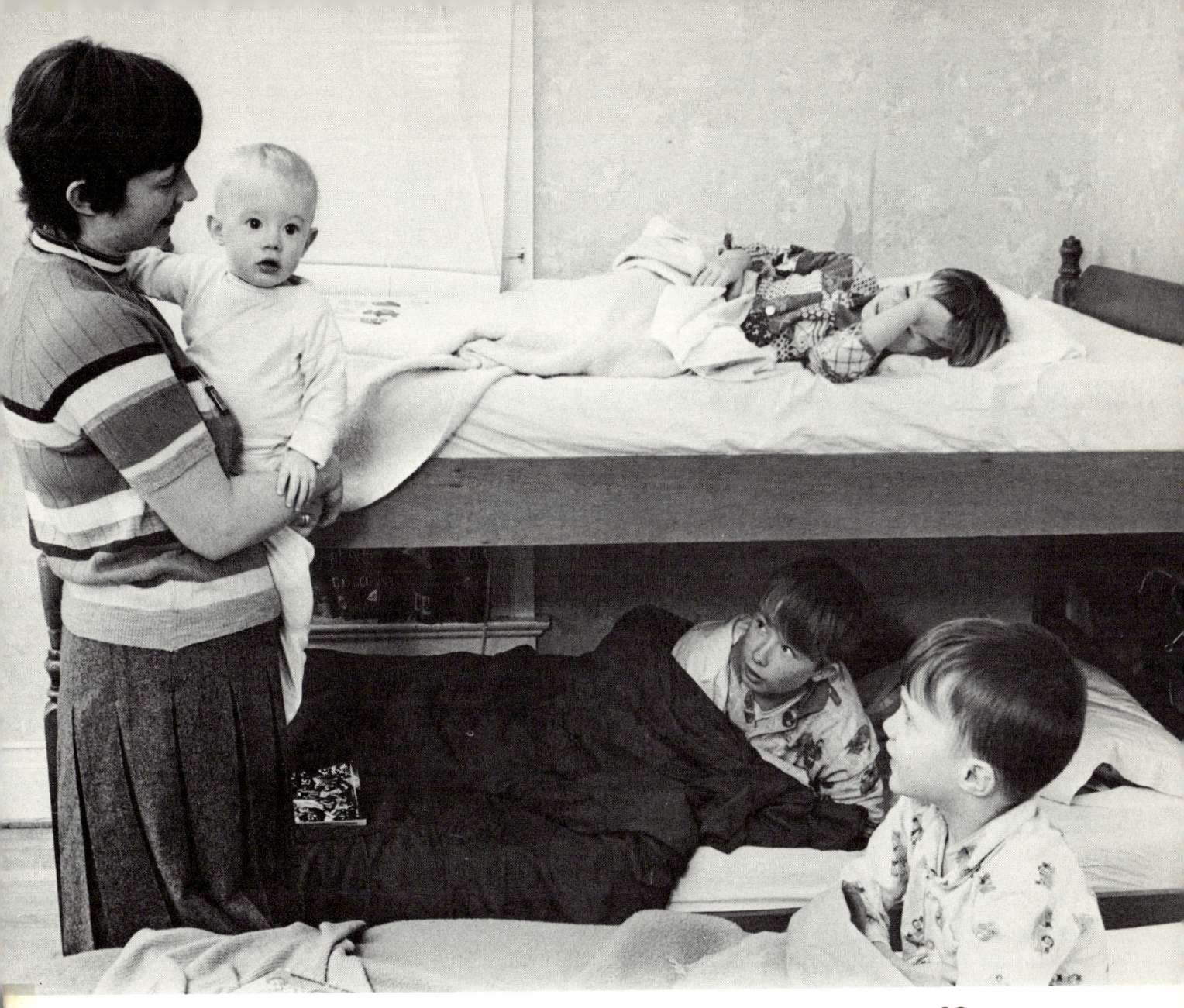

22

We must be solitaries today, so let each of you go wherever he pleases on the mountain, quite alone, weeping, singing, or praying, as God moves him.

Where hiddest thou apart,
Beloved, and left me with my anguish?
Thou fleddest like the hart;
Pierced with thy love, I languish.

In that happy night,
In secret, seen of none,
Seeing naught myself,
Without other light or guide
Save that which in my heart was burning,

That light guided me
More surely than the noonday sun
To the place where He was waiting for me,
Whom I knew well,
And where none but He appeared.

27

Let us rejoice, O my Beloved!
Let us go forth to see ourselves in Thy beauty,
To the mountain and the hill,
Where the pure water flows;
Let us enter into the heart of the thicket.
We shall go at once
to the lofty caverns of the rocks
which are all secret.
There we shall enter in
And taste of the new wine of the pomegranate.

I enter'd in—I knew not where—
And, there remaining, knew no more,
Transcending far all human lore.

I knew not where I enter'd in.
'Twas giv'n me there myself to see
And wondrous things I learn'd within,
Yet knew I not where I could be.
I'll say not what was told to me:
Remaining there, I knew no more,
Transcending far all human lore.

28

That was the love, all else above,
Of perfect peace, devotion deep.
In the profound retreat of love
The path direct I learn'd to keep.
Such secret knowledge did I reap
That, stammering, I could speak no more,
Transcending far all human lore.

30

This wond'rous knowledge knowing naught
Is of a power so sov'reign high
That wise men's reasoning and thought
Defeat it not, howe'er they try.
Ne'er can their intellect come nigh
This power of thought that thinks no more,
Transcending far all human lore.

All earthly and heavenly things are as nothing in comparison with God. . . . All the being of creatures, when compared with God's infinite Being, is nothing . . . and all the beauty of creatures, when compared with God's infinite Beauty, is supreme ugliness . . . all the goodness of earthly creatures compared with the infinite goodness of God is supreme malice.

31

God makes use of nothing else but love.

Desolation cuts sharp, but behind the darkness of suffering a great light is growing. God grant that we walk not in darkness.

When a soul has determined to turn to God and serve Him alone, He usually caresses it . . . as a loving mother does her tender child, warming it at her breast, nourishing it with her milk, and with sweet and delicate foods, bearing it about in her arms, and covering it with caresses. . . . In a short time, there will be no more milk, the soft food of children; bread with its crust instead . . . the food of the strong.

The tree that is cultivated and kept with the favor of its owner gives in due season the fruit that is expected of it.

It is vain to distress oneself even if everything is perishing, decaying, and going wrong, for such distress brings more harm than good. But, to bear all things with peaceful and tranquil equanimity not only brings much good to the soul but also enables it to judge with greater clearness and apply a suitable remedy.

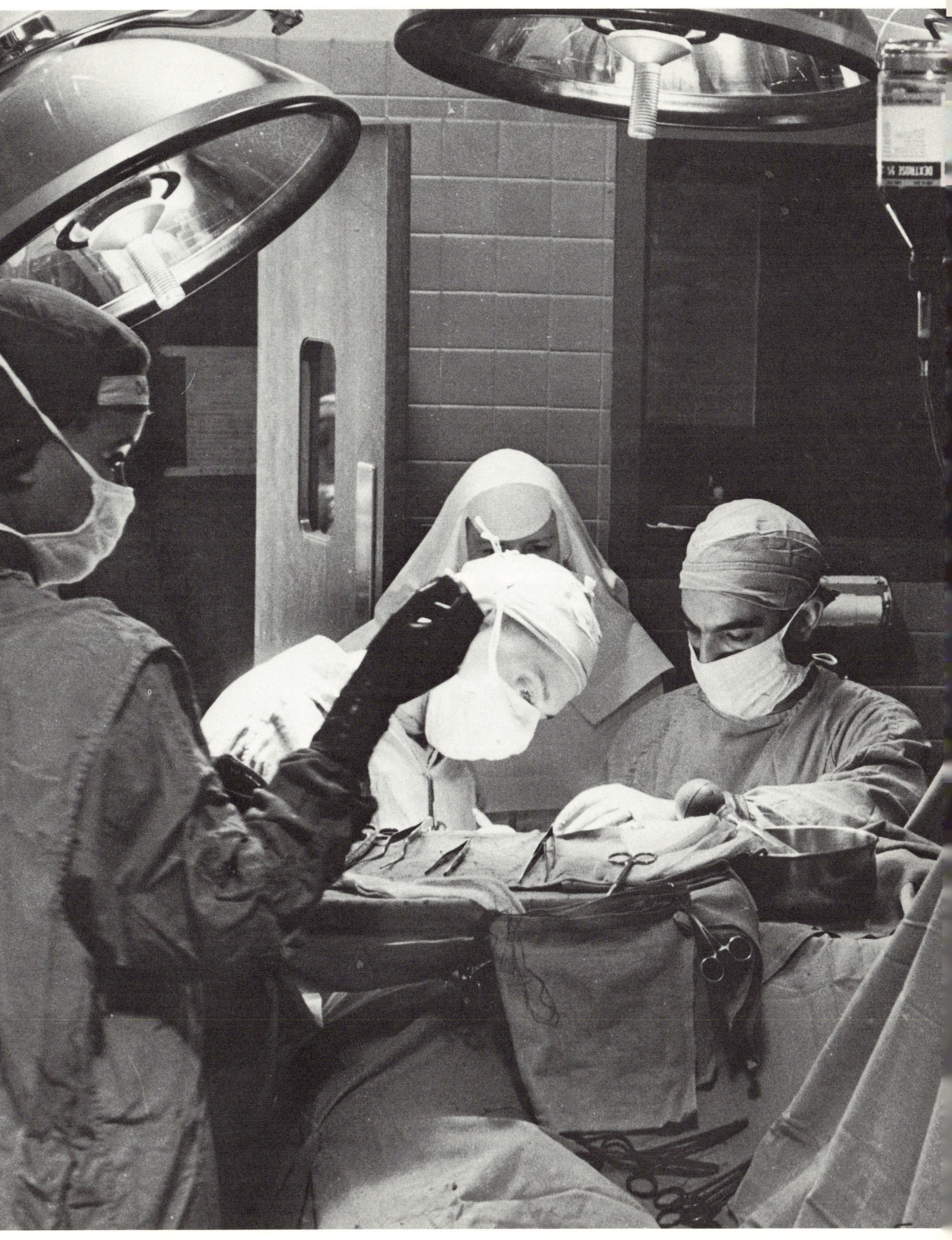

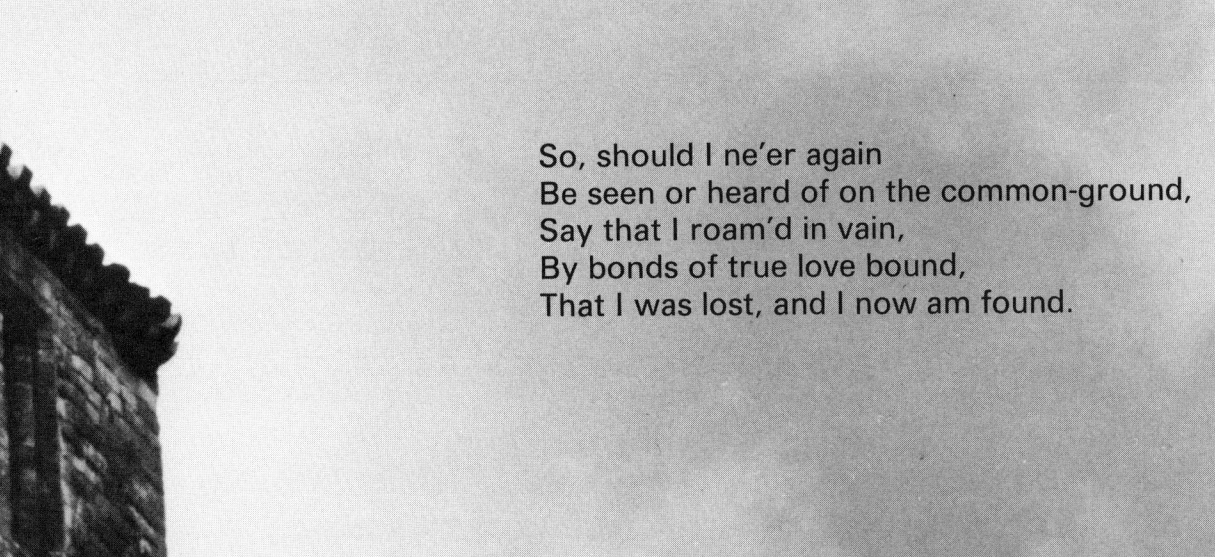

So, should I ne'er again
Be seen or heard of on the common-ground,
Say that I roam'd in vain,
By bonds of true love bound,
That I was lost, and I now am found.

O woods and thickets   Planted by the hand of the Beloved!
O meadow of verdure, enamelled with flowers, Say if he has passed by you.

Scattering a thousand graces, He passed through these groves in haste,

And, looking upon them as he went,   Left them, by His glance alone, clothed with beauty.

How is it that men say Thou art absent?

ST. JOHN OF THE CROSS

Juan de Yepes was born at Fontiveros, a village in Old Castile, in 1542. As a young man he worked as a carpenter, tailor and painter, before joining the Carmelite order, in which he was professed in 1564 and ordained in 1567. It was in that same year that he met St. Teresa of Avila and, soon after, now as John of the Cross, joined her in the Reform of the order which she had undertaken with the hope of returning it to a more primitive Rule stressing prayer and contemplation. By 1577, that Reform was meeting with such violent hostility that John was kidnapped by the Calced Carmelites and imprisoned in Toledo.

It was during his nearly nine months there, months in which he was cruelly treated, beaten and pressured to renounce the Reform, that he began to write the great lyrical works—notably the *Spiritual Canticle* and the *Dark Night of the Soul*—that nearly four centuries later continue to be recognized as among the foremost mystical poetry of all time.

Following a dramatic escape—complete with ropes made from the strips of a blanket—John resumed his work with the Discalced Carmelites, becoming superior at the convent of Calvario, where he undertook his major mystical commentaries, *The Ascent of Mount Carmel* and the *Dark Night,* which eventually were to be followed by those of the *Spiritual Canticle* and *The Living Flame of Love.*

In the years that followed, John was to serve as prior in Granada and Segovia and provincial in Andalusia. When Christ appeared to him on one occasion, John requested: "What I wish You to give me are sufferings to be borne for Your sake, and that I may be despised and regarded as worthless." His desire was granted and, in 1591, true to his prediction—"I shall be thrown into a corner"—he was deprived of his offices and sent to La Penüela, where he soon fell ill. John of the Cross died in Ubeda on December 14, 1591. He was beatified in 1675 and canonized in 1726. Pope Pius XI declared him a Doctor of the Universal Church on August 24, 1926.

PHOTO CREDITS

1. Catharine Hughes
2. Joel Edelson
3. Joel Edelson
4. Joel Edelson
5. Catharine Hughes
6. Maryknoll
7. Arthur Glick
8. Maryknoll
9. Maryknoll
10. Arthur Glick
11. Arthur Glick
12. Joseph Vesely
13. Joseph Vesely
14. Maryknoll
15. Catharine Hughes
16. Catharine Hughes
17. Maryknoll
18. Maryknoll
19. Catharine Hughes
20. Catharine Hughes
21. Arthur Glick
22. Maryknoll
23. Joseph Vesely
24. Arthur Glick
25. Mel Edelson
26. Catharine Hughes
27. Catharine Hughes
28. Arthur Glick
29. Catharine Hughes
30. Catharine Hughes
31. Joseph Vesely
32. Eileen Vesely
33. Catharine Hughes
34. Maryknoll
35. Maryknoll
36. Catharine Hughes
37. Joseph Vesely
38. Maryknoll
39. Sister Mary Campion Kuhn, C.S.C.
40. Catharine Hughes
41. Joseph Vesely